SRA Specific Skill Series
for Reading

Drawing Conclusions

Sixth Edition

SRA

Columbus, OH

The McGraw·Hill Companies

Cover: © Photodisc/Getty Images, Inc.

SRAonline.com

Mc Graw Hill **SRA**

Printed in the United States of America.

Send all inquiries to:
SRA/McGraw-Hill
8787 Orion Place
Columbus, OH 43240-4027

ISBN 0-07-604024-0

2 3 4 5 6 7 8 9 BCH 12 11 10 09 08 07 06

PURPOSE:

DRAWING CONCLUSIONS helps develop one of the most important interpretive skills. Students learn to look beyond the writer's literal statements to reach an unstated but logical conclusion based on those statements and sometimes their phrasing. In **DRAWING CONCLUSIONS** the correct conclusion is the most logical one for students to reach from only the information presented.

FOR WHOM:

The skill of **DRAWING CONCLUSIONS** is developed through a series of books spanning ten levels (Picture, Preparatory, A, B, C, D, E, F, G, H). The Picture Level is for students who have not acquired a basic sight vocabulary. The Preparatory Level is for students who have a basic sight vocabulary but are not yet ready for the first-grade-level book. Books A through H are appropriate for students who can read on levels one through eight, respectively.

THE NEW EDITION:

The sixth edition of the *Specific Skill Series for Reading* maintains the quality and focus that has distinguished this program for more than 40 years. A key element central to the program's success has been the unique nature of the reading selections. Fiction and nonfiction pieces about current topics have been designed to stimulate the interest of students, motivating them to use the comprehension strategies they have learned to further their reading. To keep this important aspect of the program intact, a percentage of the reading selections has been replaced in order to ensure the continued relevance of the subject material.

In addition, a significant percentage of the artwork in the program has been replaced to give the books a contemporary look. The cover photographs are designed to appeal to readers of all ages.

SESSIONS:

Short practice sessions are the most effective. It is desirable to have a practice session every day or every other day, using a few units each session.

SCORING:

Students should record their answers on the reproducible worksheets. The worksheets make scoring easier and provide uniform records of the students' work. Using worksheets also avoids consuming the exercise books.

It is important for students to know how well they are doing. For this reason, units should be scored as soon as they have been completed. Then a discussion can be held in which students justify their choices. (The *Language Activity Pages,* many of which are open-ended, do not lend themselves to an objective score; thus there are no answer keys for these pages.)

GENERAL INFORMATION ON *DRAWING CONCLUSIONS:*

The questions in **DRAWING CONCLUSIONS** do not deal with direct references; thus the answers do not use the same words as the paragraphs. In the Picture Level, the readers examine the picture for the correct answer. The Preparatory, A, and B levels contain primarily indirect references; that is, the answers are found in the paragraphs but with slightly different wording. Some easy conclusions are also included. As the books advance in challenge, there are more difficult conclusions, involving less obvious relationships. The conclusions also become more dependent on qualifying words such as *mostly, all, some,* and *only.*

In **DRAWING CONCLUSIONS** the readers are asked to find an example, note a contrast, generalize, see cause-and-effect relationships, detect a mood, see an analogy, identify a time or place relationship, make a comparison, or anticipate an outcome.

It is important that the teacher ask students to find in the paragraph the specific information relevant to the tentative conclusion. Then students must test the conclusion against the information provided. When the emphasis is placed on finding evidence to prove answers and when the students put themselves in roles of detectives, not only does their ability to draw conclusions rapidly improve, but they also have fun.

Students must know that a conclusion is a judgment made. It must be supported by strong evidence. In **DRAWING CONCLUSIONS** the correct answer is one that is either highly likely or certain.

Some alternate answer choices may be true. The answer that is accepted as correct, however, must not only be true but must also have supportive evidence in the paragraph. The clue may hinge on a single word, involve a phrase or a sentence, or encompass the paragraph as a whole.

RELATED MATERIALS:

Specific Skill Series Assessment Book provides the teacher with a pretest and a posttest for each skill at each grade level. These tests will help the teacher assess the students' performance in each of the nine comprehension skills.

When you read, you can often figure out things that the writer doesn't tell you directly. You do this by thinking about the information the author does tell you. When you figure out something the author does not state directly, you are **drawing conclusions.**

Good readers draw conclusions as they read. They use the information the writer gives them to figure out things that the writer does not say. Read this paragraph. What conclusion can you draw about when Hawaii became a state?

Hawaii and Alaska, which became states in the same year, are very different from each other. Alaska became the largest state when it joined the Union on January 3, 1959. Hawaii, the last state to join the Union, is one of the nation's smallest states.

Did you figure out that Hawaii became a state after January 3, 1959, but before January 1, 1960? You can draw this conclusion from the information the writer gives.

In this book, you will read paragraphs. After you read each paragraph, draw a conclusion about something in the paragraph. Use the information in the paragraph to figure out the correct answer.

1.   In Fredericksburg, Virginia, the townspeople celebrate an annual October holiday that dates back to colonial days. The Fredericksburg Dog Mart is a one-day carnival for dogs and their owners. The first Dog Mart was a trading day and was proposed by the Native Americans as a truce with colonists in the late 1600s. Weapons would not be carried. The colonists' hunting dogs would be exchanged for furs, gold, and crafts.

2.   You can experience the olden days at an exhibit at the Center of Science and Industry in Columbus, Ohio. The Progress exhibit lets visitors take a trip through time. You can learn about life in a small Midwestern town back in 1898. Then you can walk a few steps and travel through the same town set in the year 1962. You can meet the people of each era and see what life was like for them.

3.   Police can match a gun to any bullets fired by that gun. If the police believe they have found the gun from which a bullet was fired, they fire another bullet from the same gun and compare the markings on the two bullets. The barrel of a gun leaves telltale marks on a bullet. The police see if the marks on both bullets are identical.

4.   Would you like to go to a school that is partially underground? This is what students in some towns are doing. Because fuel for heat is so expensive, people want a school building that doesn't have to be heated as much. They build the school underground because the earth around it stays warm in winter. Big glass windows on the roof catch and keep the sun's heat.

5.   The police sometimes use an electronic microscope instead of an ordinary one. This instrument can enlarge a tiny dust particle to 100,000 times its actual size. If this microscope were big enough to enlarge a person of average size, the person would seem to be about 400 times as tall as the Empire State Building!

1. You can tell that
   (A) Native Americans still trade in Fredericksburg.
   (B) the colonists hunted with the Native Americans.
   (C) the Native Americans and colonists had quarrels.
   (D) the Native Americans made weapons for the colonists.

2. The Progress exhibit
   (A) is very old.
   (B) is one of a kind.
   (C) lets you learn about history.
   (D) makes you walk a lot.

3. The markings on bullets fired from the same gun
   (A) can't be identified.
   (B) are like fingerprints.
   (C) are in no way similar to footprints.
   (D) never match.

4. You can tell that the school
   (A) closes on cloudy days.
   (B) has happy students.
   (C) can't be seen from the ground.
   (D) has no windows in its walls.

5. The difference between an ordinary microscope and an electronic one is
   (A) size.
   (B) color.
   (C) weight.
   (D) magnifying power.

1. Why do presidents and royalty receive a 21-gun salute when they visit another nation? It is a show of friendship, not of war. In earlier days when a foreign ruler sailed into a port for a visit, both nations wanted to show that their guns were empty—they were not planning a surprise attack. So they fired their cannons into the air. Twenty-one was chosen as being three times the lucky number seven.

2. Before settlers from the East came to the western plains, the prairie dogs had their own "towns." One prairie dog town covered 25,000 square miles and housed about 400 million of these little rodents. The entrances to the prairie dogs' underground homes are mounds of mud, often a foot high, separated by 20 or 30 feet. Today prairie dog towns are smaller and harder to find.

3. Oysters are often planted in and harvested from bays. Oyster farmers use surface buoys to mark the locations of their oyster crops. Before the young oysters are planted, the farmer makes an area of bay bottom firm with shells and tiles. With enemies such as fish and other sea creatures, oysters have one chance in a million to reach adult size. Those that survive are brought up from the bottom of the bay and sold.

4. Some scientists now believe that humans can adopt a 48-hour day rather than a 24-hour day if time is not gauged. French scientists conducted an experiment with two volunteers who lived without clocks in a deep cave. After a period of time, the volunteers fell into 48-hour cycles—36 hours of work followed by 12 hours of sleep.

5. To help sell more wool, a sixteenth-century English ruler made it a law that everyone seven years of age and older must wear a cap made of wool. Anyone who did not was fined. So important was the wool business to England that, as late as 1824, it was a crime punishable by death to take sheep out of the country to be sold.

Unit 2

1. You can tell that in earlier days
    (A) no one believed in lucky numbers.
    (B) everyone carried a gun.
    (C) many presidents were shot.
    (D) rulers sometimes used surprise attacks.

2. From the story we can't tell
    (A) the size of the towns.
    (B) whether the number of towns has increased or decreased.
    (C) what the towns were like.
    (D) how old the towns are.

3. An oyster's chances of maturing are
    (A) about even.
    (B) very good.
    (C) one in a million.
    (D) more than one in a million.

4. From the story we can tell that it would be possible
    (A) to change our work hours.
    (B) to work more slowly.
    (C) for everyone to sleep in caves.
    (D) to sleep longer.

5. From the story we can tell that
    (A) English wool is superior.
    (B) wool was vital to the English economy.
    (C) English laws have always been mild.
    (D) there was little demand for wool in 1824.

1. We usually picture raindrops as tear shaped. The laws of science dictate otherwise. Small drops, with a radius of 1 millimeter or less, are actually spherical. As they fall they join with other drops. Because of the resistance of the air they're falling through, they flatten to look like hamburger buns. When they have a radius of 4.5 millimeters, they separate and become small drops again.

2. Big Ben, a famous clock tower in London, England, is actually the name of the 13-ton bell hanging inside the tower. Each of the four clock faces on the tower, one on each side, is 23 feet wide. The minute hand is 14 feet long, and the numerals are 2 feet high. The clock faces are illuminated at night so they can be seen from miles around.

3. Some people might admire an animal called the sloth. Because it is extremely slow and not very smart, you might expect that it is easily caught by larger animals. The opposite is true. The sloth hangs upside down in trees and moves so slowly that its enemies often do not notice it. Because sloths survive this way, their species has managed to stay on Earth for millions of years.

4. In the early 1800s a Dr. Mitchell suggested that our country be called Fredonia. The doctor chose the beginning of the English word **freedom** and the ending of the Latin word **colonia,** meaning colony. Thus **Fredonia** meant "a free settlement or colony." The people of Dr. Mitchell's time didn't seem to like the doctor's new name for our country. As everyone knows, America never became known as Fredonia.

5. The deep snow of winter can mean danger for people who live near rivers. To warn people who live where floods are likely to occur, scientists study the snowy land using photographs taken from satellites. The photos measure the depth and area of the snow. From these measurements scientists determine how much flooding will follow the spring thaw.

1. The air causes raindrops to
   (A) bounce off each other.
   (B) change shape.
   (C) remain round.
   (D) float.

2. Based on the reading, the reader can conclude that
   (A) the second hand is 12 feet long.
   (B) the bell is very loud.
   (C) the bell rings every hour.
   (D) the clock tower is famous only in London.

3. If sloths moved faster, they might now be
   (A) right side up.
   (B) rulers of the forest.
   (C) extinct.
   (D) far greater in number.

4. We know that Americans didn't like the name **Fredonia** because they
   (A) didn't understand Latin.
   (B) kept the name America.
   (C) didn't want freedom.
   (D) disliked Dr. Mitchell.

5. The paragraph leads you to understand that
   (A) in the future, floods may cause more damage.
   (B) satellite photos serve as flood warnings.
   (C) satellites can predict the hour a flood will start.
   (D) winter is the most dangerous season for floods.

1.   Tornadoes in the United States occur most frequently in ten states that form the boundary of the Great Plains. The land in the Great Plains is relatively flat. Cold, dry, polar air from Canada can easily meet warm, moist, tropical air from the Gulf of Mexico. Most tornadoes form along the front between the two air masses. This area is known as Tornado Alley.

2.   Thousands of people who cannot hear learn to read lips. Even people who use hearing aids find that knowing how to lip-read helps tremendously. In lipreading courses tongue and teeth positions are studied. The sounds, not the spellings, of the words are lip-read. People are given lists of words with certain sounds to practice in front of a mirror. Good lipreaders never stop practicing.

3.   One of the oldest of Roman roads was made because of people's desire for salt. This road, the Via Salaria, or salt road, ran westward from Rome to the salt beds of Ostia on the coast of Italy. Salt was carried along this ancient road. Soldiers in the army of ancient Rome were paid with salt. In fact this is how the word **salary** and the expression "worth one's salt" originated.

4.   The combination lock found on modern safes is old indeed. It was invented by the Chinese thousands of years ago. The lock consisted of a number of movable rings. Each ring was covered with letters. To open the lock it was necessary to arrange the rings so that the letters spelled a word that had been decided on in advance.

5.   Not many years ago most medicines had a bad taste. It seemed to most people that the taste of the medicine was as unpleasant as the sickness it was designed to cure. Today many medicines have a pleasing artificial flavor that can hide a bad flavor. Some have a cherry taste. Sometimes the same medicine is manufactured in different flavors.

1. Based on the reading, the reader can conclude that
   (A) tornadoes can occur anywhere that cold air masses meet warm air masses.
   (B) the two air masses take the form of a cloud.
   (C) few people live in Tornado Alley because of the tornado risk.
   (D) all tornadoes cause a lot of damage.

2. You can tell that lipreading
   (A) is exactly like a hearing aid.
   (B) can be learned by almost anyone willing to practice.
   (C) can be learned only by those who cannot hear others speak.
   (D) has to do with the spellings of the words.

3. You can tell that salt was used
   (A) as medicine.
   (B) as money.
   (C) only in Ostia.
   (D) only in eastern Italy.

4. The Chinese invented
   (A) the padlock.
   (B) secret codes.
   (C) the combination lock.
   (D) the movable ring.

5. We know that today
   (A) all medicines taste bad.
   (B) all medicines taste good.
   (C) all medicines come in many flavors.
   (D) medicines have changed.

Unit 5

1.   You may like to care for an injured canary or bluebird, but what about an eagle or a falcon? An aviary in Utah has one of the few aid stations in this country for birds of prey—large birds with sharp claws for catching and eating small animals. The aviary fixes these birds' broken bones, cleans their wounds, and feeds them vitamins.

2.   Varnish is a liquid used to protect wooden surfaces from the damaging effects of air and moisture. Varnish also improves the appearance of a surface by giving it a smooth, glossy finish. Well-applied coats have been known to remain smooth and unscratched for centuries. Egyptian rulers' mummy cases, removed from ancient tombs, remain almost unchanged 3,000 years after varnish was applied.

3.   The Romans thought highly of chickens for all important matters. A priest wrote the letters of the alphabet on the ground in a circle and placed a grain of wheat on each letter. Then a chicken was put in the center. The priest carefully watched from which letters the chicken took the wheat grains and "read" the bird's choices as good or bad signs.

4.   What standard is used to set clocks in the United States? In the Naval Observatory Building near Washington, D.C., is a master clock. It is located in an airtight, dustproof, glass-enclosed chamber. The floor is eight inches thick so that nothing will jar the clock. All clocks in the United States are set from this master clock.

5.   In 1719 a man named Rene de Réaumur noticed that wasps' nests were made of a fine gray paper. He discovered that wasps chewed on bits of rotten wood. They mixed the bits of wood fiber with chemicals in their saliva. From this wood pulp the wasps made paper nests. Réaumur had discovered the wasps' secret—that paper could be made from wood without the use of rags.

Unit 5

1. You can tell that the aviary
   (A) is in a large city.
   (B) takes care of canaries and bluebirds.
   (C) takes care of birds that hunt.
   (D) is a zoo.

2. One of the most important things about varnish is its
   (A) long-lasting quality.
   (B) variety of colors.
   (C) stickiness.
   (D) cheapness.

3. You can tell that
   (A) chance played a major role in important Roman matters.
   (B) all the letters were the same.
   (C) the chicken learned to read the letters.
   (D) the Romans were superstitious.

4. The author implies that
   (A) clocks are easily thrown off time.
   (B) dust is good for clocks.
   (C) clocks must be set on a level floor.
   (D) little use is made of the master clock.

5. From the story you can tell that
   (A) Mr. Réaumur was observant.
   (B) wasps are the same as bees.
   (C) Mr. Réaumur was a beekeeper.
   (D) paper is manufactured with saliva.

1.   English women once thought they looked best with wigs that rose two or even three feet above their heads. Wool, cotton, and goats' hair were used to give the hairpieces the desired height. The finest high-piled wigs were often decorated with imitation fruit, model ships, model horses, and figurines.

2.   Though Americans take pride in the accomplishments of the Pony Express, few people know of an earlier and equally remarkable postal service. In the fifteenth and sixteenth centuries, messages traveled 150 miles a day—without the aid of a horse! Inca Indian runners were spaced about three miles apart over a stone road that stretched 5,000 miles. These relay runners were the "express mail" carriers of their time.

3.   When a large number of soldiers march across a small bridge, they are usually told to break step. If the bridge isn't particularly strong and the soldiers march in step, they can start a vibration that can cause the bridge to collapse. That is also the main reason trains go slowly across bridges. A faster motion could produce vibrations and increase the danger of a bridge disaster.

4.   The liver is the largest of the body's glands. It helps the body absorb nutrients by producing a fluid that breaks down the food taken into the body. The liver keeps a close watch on the bloodstream, clearing the blood of many harmful products. The liver also stores sugar for future use and makes sure the heart does not become overloaded with blood.

5.   By actually fishing for and catching other fish, the anglerfish grows to be almost four feet long. It lies quietly in mud at the bottom of the water. Three wormlike "fingers" on top of its head attract other fish. When the fish come close, the anglerfish gets its meal. If fishing is slow, the anglerfish might rise to the surface and swallow ducks or other swimming birds.

1. From the story you cannot tell
   (A) how wigs were decorated.
   (B) how high the wigs were.
   (C) what the wigs were made of.
   (D) the color of the wigs.

2. The best nickname for these Inca messengers would be
   (A) Pony Express.
   (B) Inca Express.
   (C) 800-year Mail.
   (D) Horseless Carriage.

3. Trains go slowly across bridges
   (A) because bridges are long.
   (B) because trains are long.
   (C) for more than one reason.
   (D) because some bridges are weak.

4. The liver performs
   (A) one function.
   (B) two functions.
   (C) four functions.
   (D) three functions.

5. You can conclude that anglerfish
   (A) prefer fish to other animals.
   (B) have worms growing out of their heads.
   (C) are often eaten by birds.
   (D) always remain at the bottom of the water.

The First L A P
Language Activity Pages

A. Exercising Your Skill

Do you enjoy riddles? Did you ever stop to think that when you solve a riddle, you are really drawing a conclusion? A conclusion is a decision or judgment you make based on facts and information. Read the following riddles, and think about the information each one contains. Write the answers on your paper.

1. Do you say, "Seven and five is thirteen," or "Seven and five are thirteen"?

2. If you were hiking along a mountain trail in western Canada and saw a grizzly bear waking up from a long nap, what time would it be?

3. What was the highest mountain before Mt. Everest was discovered?

4. What is as big as an elephant but doesn't weigh anything?

5. Which month is the shortest?

6. Where can you always find health, wealth, and happiness?

7. What has a head but no brain?

8. What word is always pronounced incorrectly?

9. What can you add to a bucket of water that will make it weigh less?

10. How can you go without sleep for seven days and not get tired?

B. Expanding Your Skill

Take turns asking and answering the riddles. Did everyone come up with the same answers? Discuss the information given in each riddle that led to your answers. Then turn this page upside down to check the answers to the riddles.

Answers: 1. Neither. Seven and five are twelve; **2.** time to run; **3.** Mt. Everest; **4.** the elephant's shadow; **5.** May; **6.** in the dictionary; **7.** lettuce, cabbage, cauliflower; **8.** the word incorrectly; **9.** holes; **10.** sleep at night

C. Exploring Language

What makes a joke funny? To understand the humor of a joke, you need to draw conclusions about it. Read each of the following jokes. On your paper answer the questions about the jokes.

1. Kanisha asked her teacher, "Would you scold someone for something she didn't do?"
   "Of course not," her teacher answered. "Why do you ask?"
   "Because I didn't do my math homework," Kanisha answered.

What did the teacher mean when she said that she wouldn't scold someone for something she didn't do? Tell the class.

2. A traveler asked the ticket agent at a railroad station for a round-trip ticket.
   "Where to?" the ticket agent asked.
   "Back to here," the traveler said.

What did the ticket agent want to know? Tell the class.

3. Willy asked Billy, "Were you born in New York?"
   "Yes," Billy answered.
   "What part?" asked Willy.
   "All of me," said Billy.

What did Willy want to know? Tell the class.

D. Expressing Yourself

Choose one of these activities.

1. Create riddles of your own to ask your classmates. See whether they can guess the answers to your riddles by using the information you provide. Have them explain how they arrived at the answers.

2. Play 20 Questions with your classmates. The leader thinks of an object. The others ask questions that can be answered only with *Yes* or *No.* Then they put the clues together to draw a conclusion about the object.

3. Tell jokes to the rest of the class. If you don't know any jokes, you can find them in a library book. Have your classmates tell what is funny about the jokes.

1. The city of Minneapolis was named by Charles Hoag. In 1852 this little frontier village needed a name. Mr. Hoag decided to take the Native American word for the nearby falls, **Minnehaha,** and combine it with the Greek word **polis,** meaning "city." He put them together, made some changes, and created **Minneapolis.** The name caught on with the settlers.

2. Big Bend National Park in Texas is one of the largest and least visited national parks in America. It includes more than 801,000 acres of deep canyons, vast deserts, and the entire Chisos Mountain range. The park is very large and remote. The nearest town is 100 miles away. The park is named for the U-turn bend in the Rio Grande River.

3. Many common idioms, or figures of speech, come from the horse world. *Don't put the cart before the horse* is a phrase that means you should not do things in the wrong order. When someone is *on his high horse,* he is being arrogant and self-righteous. If you have tried to help someone who would not help herself, you might say, *you can lead a horse to water but you can't make her drink.*

4. If you have ever been in the southern United States, you may have experienced fire ants at work. Some fire ants are native to the United States. But pest fire ants were accidental. They arrived on ships from South America into Mobile, Alabama, and then spread throughout the South. Fire ants are small, reddish-brown or black ants that are extremely aggressive and sting relentlessly.

5. If somebody asked you, "What animal might you see climbing a coconut tree?" you would probably answer, "A monkey." However, you would be just as correct if you answered, "A crab." The large robber crab climbs coconut trees by wrapping its long legs around the trunk.

1. The word **Minneapolis**
   (A) came about by pure chance.
   (B) was liked by the Native Americans.
   (C) came from two languages.
   (D) is less than 100 years old.

2. At Big Bend National Park, there are probably many
   (A) restaurants.
   (B) police officers.
   (C) skiers.
   (D) wild animals.

3. From the reading you can tell that idioms
   (A) come from life experiences.
   (B) come from England.
   (C) are sayings used only by children.
   (D) don't make a lot of sense.

4. From the paragraph you know that fire ants are
   (A) harmless.
   (B) from Japan.
   (C) something to avoid.
   (D) fascinating to watch.

5. From the story you cannot tell
   (A) whether robber crabs can live outside of water.
   (B) whether robber crabs eat coconuts.
   (C) how robber crabs climb trees.
   (D) whether robber crabs are large.

1.   Some artisans make stones into usable or decorative items. They are called lapidaries. Lapidary artists work with minerals, stones, and gemstones. They also work with other materials such as bone, shell, and amber. Lapidaries use a variety of tools such as rock saws, grinders, and files. They use the tools to cut, shape, and polish stones. Other tools are used to carve designs in the stones.

2.   Berries called rose hips became an important food in Great Britain during World War II. At that time oranges and lemons—a major source of vitamin C for the British people—were in short supply. Rose hips, however, were rich in vitamin C and were available. The government encouraged the manufacture and sale of rose hip syrup, a product that is still sold.

3.   Chimpanzees are intrigued by watches and clocks. They enjoy holding a clock up to their ear and listening to it tick. This interest is so strong that chimps have been known to pick up a picture of a clock from a magazine and try to listen to it. On occasion when a chimp is holding a clock that starts to ring, it will flee in panic!

4.   Canada is rich in natural resources. About five percent of its land is suitable for farming. Canadian fishing grounds are extremely productive. Canada is among the chief producers of lead, zinc, copper, gold, nickel, and uranium. With a vast forest area covering more than one million square miles and a wealth of fur-bearing animals, Canada relies on its natural resources for a large portion of the country's exports.

5.   Hummingbirds must eat almost constantly to live. Once, seven hummingbirds shipped to New York were sped by taxi to the Bronx Zoo. It was only a half-hour trip, but it proved too long for the hungry birds. By the time they reached the zoo, five had become unconscious from hunger, and one had died.

1. Lapidary artists probably make
   (A) tools.
   (B) jewelry.
   (C) belts.
   (D) silverware.

2. The story shows that the British government was
   (A) eager to make money.
   (B) afraid of losing the war.
   (C) unwilling to import oranges and lemons.
   (D) concerned about its citizens' health.

3. You can tell that chimpanzees
   (A) recognize timepieces.
   (B) are interested in time.
   (C) can tell time.
   (D) are mystified by time.

4. The story mentions
   (A) no resources.
   (B) six metals.
   (C) 12 major resources.
   (D) 20 major resources.

5. The hummingbirds were rushed to the zoo because
   (A) it was late.
   (B) they were ill.
   (C) the zoo was closing.
   (D) they needed to be fed.

1.   The willow grows better beside America's rivers than any other kind of tree. The Mississippi River is bordered by willows for a distance of more than 2,500 miles. Dwarf willows grow well along mountain streams and along riverbanks in the dry plains of the West. These trees can live with their roots unprotected by soil. Willows that tumble into rivers and wash downstream can even put down their roots and grow again.

2.   Certain worker bees are in charge of cleaning the wax cells that will contain honey and larvae. When a bee has died inside the hive, the workers carry the dead bee far away. These bees also seal and repair the cells with propolis, or bee glue, a mixture of tree resin, saliva, and beeswax. Propolis is sterile and acts like an antibiotic, thus preventing the spread of disease.

3.   Domestic rabbits are direct descendants of the wild European rabbit. The domestic rabbit looks quite different from its wild cousins. However, its behavior is very much the same. Rabbits are prey animals. This means that other animals eat them for food. Domestic rabbits still think and act like prey animals. They are fearful even as pets. They make almost no noise and generally do not like to be picked up.

4.   The first national park to be established in the United States east of the Mississippi River is known as Acadia National Park. The park, located in Maine, covers more than 47,000 acres on Mount Desert Island, Isle au Haut, and on Schoodic Peninsula. A spectacular view is provided from the peak of Mount Cadillac. Acadia National Park is also an excellent sanctuary for wildlife.

5.   Is blown glass an art or a craft? Artist Dale Chihuly is at the center of that debate. Glass has traditionally been a material for making usable items. Fine art is art that is intended for beauty or interest, not for utility. Glassblowing has long been considered a craft rather than a fine art. But Dale Chihuly is one artist who is changing that idea. He makes art from blown glass. Its only purpose is to be interesting and beautiful.

1. From the paragraph you can tell
  (A) the height of a willow tree.
  (B) where willow trees grow well.
  (C) the shape of a willow tree.
  (D) where willow trees are never found.

2. Bees are very much concerned with their
  (A) color.
  (B) flowers.
  (C) mummies.
  (D) health.

3. From the paragraph you know that rabbits might not be
  (A) very intelligent.
  (B) nice to other rabbits.
  (C) the ideal pet for everyone.
  (D) as big as wild rabbits.

4. The writer hints that
  (A) Mount Cadillac was named after an automobile.
  (B) Acadia was America's first national park.
  (C) earlier parks were established west of the Mississippi.
  (D) there is little animal life in the park.

5. You can conclude from the paragraph that
  (A) art can be made from anything.
  (B) art is expensive.
  (C) glass is not art.
  (D) Dale Chihuly is an artist from long ago.

1.	In 1855 in Worcester, Massachusetts, Joseph Stoddard invented a steam-powered organ. Its music could be heard ten miles away. The inventor decided to call this wonderful organ a calliope. **Kalliope,** in Greek, means "beautiful voiced." Today we can still hear the calliope at carnivals and fairs. The sound may not always be beautiful, but no one can say that it isn't loud and different.

2.	"Red sky at night, sailors delight; Red sky in the morning, sailors take warning" is an old proverb that warns of rain. Actually there is a reason this proverb about the color of the sky was so widespread. A red sun indicates that dust and moisture are in the air. These are two of the important elements necessary for rain. Thus, the proverb has some scientific validity.

3.	The Charter Oak was a famous tree in Hartford, Connecticut. In 1687 the government of England appointed an administrator to take away the charter and freedom of the Connecticut colony. A charter is a document listing certain rights and obligations. According to tradition, the charter was hidden in an oak tree to keep the English from seizing it. Years later winds destroyed this huge tree. Today a monument marks the spot where the tree stood.

4.	Most snow avalanches make very little noise as they hurtle down mountainsides. Only a slight hissing sound can be heard. Large chunks of snow, however, make a dull, thudding sound as they go over cliffs. An ice avalanche has a sharper sound, more like thunder. An airborne powder avalanche, on the other hand, hums, whistles, and whines as it makes its descent.

5.	The idea for contact lenses is as old as Leonardo da Vinci. He sketched and described them in 1508. But contact lenses did not become a reality until the end of the nineteenth century. The first contact lenses were made of glass. They were hard, uncomfortable, and few people could afford them. Today contact lenses are made of soft plastics. They come in a variety of colors. Some contacts can be worn overnight or even for several days.

1. You can tell that the inventor
    (A) didn't take long to build the calliope.
    (B) must have been deaf.
    (C) liked the sound the calliope made.
    (D) was a very musical person.

2. You can tell that
    (A) there is no truth to this proverb.
    (B) other elements are also important for rain.
    (C) rain doesn't need moisture or dust.
    (D) sailors like red in the morning.

3. A good name for the Charter Oak would be
    (A) Yum-Yum Tree.
    (B) Old Oaken Bucket.
    (C) Freedom's Friend.
    (D) Friendly Chestnut Tree.

4. During a snow avalanche, people
    (A) hear a great amount of noise.
    (B) hear no sound at all.
    (C) most likely hear a hissing sound.
    (D) most likely hear a thunderous sound.

5. Today's contact lenses are
    (A) very expensive.
    (B) commonplace.
    (C) made of glass.
    (D) unsafe to wear.

1. The armadillo is the state mammal of Texas. It is an armored, insect-eating mammal, about the size of a cat. It is shaped like an anteater and has a bony, scaled shell that protects it from other animals. Armadillos are great diggers. Because they dig many burrows and they dig for food, armadillos cannot live where the soil is too hard to dig.

2. Can volcanoes affect our weather? In 1815 a huge volcano erupted in the Java Sea. The next summer was an unusually cold one in North America, and people were puzzled by the low temperatures. Today many scientists think they know what happened. They believe that dust from the volcano spread into the atmosphere, screened the sun, and prevented its heat from reaching Earth.

3. Rats destroy buildings by digging beneath the foundations. The weakened buildings collapse. Rats cause floods by digging through dams. They have been known to start fires by gnawing through the protective covering of electric wires. By running across open switches and creating short circuits, rats have brought telephone communication to a halt.

4. The polar bear is one of the cleverest hunters in the animal kingdom. It will swim beneath the ice to a place near a seal's escape hole. The bear then raps on the underside of the ice. Alarmed, the seal dives into the water. Waiting for it is the crafty and hungry bear!

5. The United States doesn't have many date groves. It is more profitable to use land for houses and factories. However, Arizona and Southern California have a few groves. The National Date Festival, which originated in Indio, California, attracts more than 270,000 visitors during the third week of February. There are camel races, horse shows, and many date-flavored foods such as ice cream and milk shakes.

1. From the paragraph, you can conclude that
   (A) all Texans love armadillos.
   (B) armadillos have no natural enemy.
   (C) armadillos can be destructive.
   (D) armadillos are charming animals.

2. The story suggests that the connection between volcanoes and weather
   (A) is based on a legend.
   (B) became clear in 1815.
   (C) is likely but not certain.
   (D) may explain all unusual weather.

3. The story mentions
   (A) one way rats help us.
   (B) two ways rats cause trouble.
   (C) six ways rats cause trouble.
   (D) four ways rats cause trouble.

4. The writer suggests that the polar bear
   (A) knows the habits of the seal.
   (B) digs escape holes for seals.
   (C) is the biggest animal.
   (D) is a better swimmer than a seal.

5. From the story you cannot tell
   (A) why there are few date groves in the United States.
   (B) when the date festival occurs.
   (C) where most date groves are.
   (D) how many dates are sold.

1.   If you were trying to fall asleep, would a dark, quiet room be the best place to go? French scientists have found that a boring situation brings on sleep better than darkness and silence. In this experiment people who experienced the tiresome repeating of sound or light fell asleep more easily than people in quiet darkness. The next time you can't get to sleep, listen to the faucet drip or watch the corner traffic light.

2.   Almost no plants can survive in the bone-dry soil of Africa's Sahara Desert. Yet cave paintings from 6,000 years ago in southern Algeria show farmers grazing cattle on rich grasslands. Changes in climate and the failure of people to be careful of soil and water supplies turned the pastureland to desert. The Sahara continues to spread southward each year.

3.   A school in Spirit Lake, Iowa, uses the wind for electricity. The school has a wind turbine on site. It provides more electricity than the school can use. The school sells the extra power to an energy company. It earned $25,000 in less than eight years. The school uses electricity from the utility company when the wind does not blow.

4.   Some of the tricks played by tornadoes seem unbelievable. One tornado whisked all the feathers from a chicken, leaving the animal embarrassed but otherwise unharmed. Another snatched the covers off a surprised sleeper. Still other tornadoes have carried mirrors for miles, leaving them undamaged, without as much as a single crack!

5.   Few animals can leap like the kangaroo. A full-grown kangaroo can make jumps of up to 30 feet. It can also clear fences eight feet high. Even when an enemy catches up with it, the kangaroo is a difficult opponent. The kangaroo is also an excellent boxer, using its front paws. Its powerful tail can cause great damage too.

1. People who are trying to stay awake should
   (A) watch a slowly blinking light.
   (B) listen to a repeated sound.
   (C) read an exciting book.
   (D) read a dull book.

2. The writer does not suggest that
   (A) cave paintings give information about the past.
   (B) more rain used to fall in the region of the Sahara.
   (C) southern Algeria is in the Sahara Desert.
   (D) people can change the Sahara back to farmland.

3. The school is unusual because
   (A) it has a wind turbine on site.
   (B) it uses electricity.
   (C) it is in Iowa.
   (D) it paid for electricity.

4. You can tell that tornadoes
   (A) don't occur very often.
   (B) are always harmful.
   (C) never do any harm.
   (D) can cause strange things to happen.

5. The number of defenses listed for a kangaroo is
   (A) two.
   (B) three.
   (C) four.
   (D) five.

A. Exercising Your Skill

An analogy is a way of comparing things. When we make an analogy, we are saying that things that are otherwise unlike are similar in some way. We are pointing out a relationship between two sets of things. For example:

Pitcher is to **baseball** as **quarterback** is to **football.**

In other words a pitcher is one of the players in a baseball game, just as a quarterback is one of the players in a football game.

Analogies may show many different kinds of relationships. They may relate words with similar meanings (synonyms), words with opposite meanings (antonyms), parts to the whole, users to things used, or actions to objects.

Read each item below, and draw a conclusion about the relationship between the sets of things. Ask yourself whether there is a relationship between the two sets of things. For each analogy write *Yes* or *No* on your paper to tell whether you think the analogy makes sense.

1. The **moon** is to **Earth** as **Earth** is to the **sun.**

2. **Puzzle** is to **solution** as **lock** is to **key.**

3. **Needles** are to **pine tree** as **leaves** are to **autumn.**

4. **Reality** is to **fantasy** as **pleasure** is to **enjoyment.**

5. **Gray** is to **black** as **pink** is to **red.**

6. **Ship** is to **port** as **car** is to **garage.**

7. **Row** is to **boat** as **pedal** is to **bicycle.**

8. **Fox** is to **den** as **grizzly** is to **bear.**

9. **Pod** is to **pea** as **shell** is to **walnut.**

10. **Scissors** are to **sharp** as **stapler** is to **staple.**

B. Expanding Your Skill

Discuss the analogies with your classmates. For each analogy that made sense, explain the relationship between the two sets of things. For each analogy that did not make sense, explain why there is no relationship. Then rewrite the incorrect analogies so they make sense.

C. Exploring Language

To supply the missing word in an analogy, draw a conclusion about the relationship between the words in the complete pair. Then supply a word that has the same relationship to the remaining word. Remember that the relationship between the words in each pair must be similar and that the items in each pair must be in the same order.

Read each of the following incomplete analogies. On your paper write the word that correctly completes each analogy.

1. **Valuable** is to **precious** as **worthless** is to _____.

2. **Poodle** is to _____ as **Siamese** is to **cat**.

3. _____ is to **firefighter** as **hammer** is to **carpenter**.

4. **Numbers** are to **mathematics** as _____ are to **language**.

5. **Above** is to _____ as **front** is to **back**.

6. **Strings** are to **guitar** as _____ are to **piano**.

7. **Flock** is to **geese** as _____ is to **horses**.

8. _____ is to **state** as **state** is to **country**.

9. **Fawn** is to **deer** as _____ is to **cow**.

10. **Rainbow trout** is to _____ as **eagle** is to **bird**.

D. Expressing Yourself

Choose one of these activities.

1. Create your own analogies based on your favorite story characters, athletes, or entertainers from television, music, or movies. Share your analogies with your classmates. Make sure you can explain the relationships within the analogies.

2. Write an analogy of your own based on each kind of relationship listed below. Look back at the analogies in Part C for examples if you need help.

   - Antonyms
   - Item to category
   - Part to whole
   - Synonyms
   - Animal to its young

1.   Often the history of a word gives a clue to its meaning, but sometimes the original meaning no longer applies. Back in Roman times, four of the months were named for the order in which they occurred. **September, October, November,** and **December** meant "seventh," "eighth," "ninth," and "tenth," respectively.

2.   Many people mistakenly think that a camel's hump is used to store water for long desert travel. This is not true. Camels' humps are food storehouses. They are made of fat, which is stored energy, just as in human bodies. When other food sources are scarce, a camel can absorb energy from its hump. As it does so, the hump shrinks.

3.   Earthquakes are often classified into three groups. Normal or shallow earthquakes, which originate somewhere between Earth's surface and 43 miles beneath it, are the most common type. Quakes that start between 43 and 186 miles beneath the surface are classified as intermediate earthquakes. Those that originate deeper than 186 miles are called deep earthquakes.

4.   In the southern United States during early colonial days, there were very few towns and thus, very few inns. Travelers didn't have many places to stay. Planters, separated by great distances from their neighbors, led lonely lives. They were always glad to see new faces. Sometimes they stationed servants at places where a traveler might pass to extend an invitation for a meal or a night's lodging.

5.   The Merino sheep is a champion producer of wool. It is covered with fleece from its nose to its tail. A large Merino may produce as much as 30 pounds of wool. This is enough to make cloth for 11 high-quality woolen suits. The amount of wool from the shearing of one Merino ram, spun into a single thread, would stretch from Chicago to New York!

1. From the paragraph you can conclude that
   (A) the Romans did not have a calendar.
   (B) December was the 12th month of the Roman calendar.
   (C) our calendar is different from the Roman calendar.
   (D) **September** meant "second."

2. You can conclude from the information that
   (A) a camel's hump expands when it eats.
   (B) a camel's hump shrinks when the camel is thirsty.
   (C) camels never need to drink water at all.
   (D) camels can find food only in the desert.

3. Earthquakes are often classified by
   (A) the amount of damage they cause.
   (B) their point of origin.
   (C) their noise.
   (D) their size.

4. Planters of early colonial times probably
   (A) were afraid.
   (B) were self-sufficient.
   (C) were never alone.
   (D) had many friends.

5. From the story you can't tell
   (A) what is made from Merino wool.
   (B) why the Merino is a champion wool producer.
   (C) why Merino sheep are valued.
   (D) how much a Merino sheep weighs.

1.   In an old-time "aerodrome" in Old Rhinebeck, New York, people can imagine themselves back in World War I. Small wood-and-wire planes buzz skyward to act out the air fights of 1917. These creations look fragile compared with today's jets, but their ability to move about easily is amazing. One plane dives straight down at another plane that suddenly dips and slips away sideways. Monoplanes, biplanes, and triplanes are kept here in perfect working condition.

2.   There is no such thing as a perfect clock. Some run fast, and others run slow. But the closest thing to perfection is the atomic clock. It is so accurate that scientists predict it will lose only one second in 200,000 years. Unfortunately it is not for sale at the corner store. This clock is designed for scientific use and costs more than $50,000!

3.   Certain hurricanes are called "hundred-year storms," meaning there is only a slight chance (one percent) that such storms would happen any given day. Hurricanes Hugo and Andrew, in 1989 and 1992, respectively, were "hundred-year storms." Meteorologists wonder what is happening. They suspect that global warming, which is the result of increased burning of fossil fuels, might be making storms more violent.

4.   People drive long distances to see the Painted Desert in Arizona. The desert is best viewed at sunrise and sunset, when the colors are the most brilliant and the shadows are the deepest. Minerals in the sand reflect the sun's rays and make the Painted Desert one of the most exciting sights in the Southwest.

5.   Anagrams are made by rearranging the letters in a word or group of words so that they spell a different word or phrase. The letters can be arranged in any order, not just reversed. For example, the letters in the word **rat** may be rearranged to spell **tar.** An anagram for **astronomer** could be **moon starer.**

1. You can tell that in 1917
   (A) travel by airplanes was common.
   (B) airplanes were better than modern jets.
   (C) World War I was being fought.
   (D) a battle was fought at the aerodrome.

2. The perfect clock
   (A) has not yet been invented.
   (B) is in common use.
   (C) can be purchased in the United States.
   (D) is the sundial.

3. You can conclude from the paragraph that
   (A) people are angry at weather predictions.
   (B) hurricanes Hugo and Andrew were a century apart.
   (C) global warming is caused by severe hurricanes.
   (D) meteorologists speculate about today's weather patterns.

4. The Painted Desert is probably most attractive
   (A) when it is cloudy.
   (B) at midday.
   (C) at twilight.
   (D) at midnight.

5. An example of a word and its anagram is
   (A) return—comeback.
   (B) sail—sole.
   (C) renew—newer.
   (D) small—tall.

1.   May 20, 1873, marks the date denim blue jeans were patented. Earlier, around 1853, Levi Strauss traveled from New York to California. His goal was to sell canvas that would be used for wagon and tent covers. At the time, however, he discovered a demand for sturdy pants. The original pants he created were made of canvas. There were many complaints that the pants were uncomfortable, so Levi later used another sturdy yet softer cotton material from Genoa, Italy. He later coined this material "jeans."

2.   Mystic, Connecticut, is a rebuilt colonial seaport and shipbuilding center. Here at the river's edge you can see the *Charles W. Morgan,* the last remaining wooden whaling ship. You can also see the *Australia,* a 75-foot, two-masted schooner that is the oldest American schooner afloat. The shops, stores, and cobblestone streets also help remind visitors of life during the days of the great sailing ships.

3.   In 279 B.C. a king named Pyrrhus won an important battle. The fight, however, cost him so many soldiers and officers that his army was seriously weakened. Joyless in his win, King Pyrrhus said, "One more such victory and we are lost." Indeed, in the end he lost the war. Today such a victory is often called a "Pyrrhic victory."

4.   The unit used to measure distance traveled over water is called the nautical mile. It is equal to 6,076 feet. The statute mile, 5,280 feet, is a unit of land measurement. Clearly the distance is not the same. When we use the word **mile,** we should be certain that the listener knows which kind of mile we are talking about.

5.   Many women in ancient times used cosmetics. Cleopatra painted her eyebrows and lashes black, just as many women do today. She painted her upper lids blue-black and the lower ones green. Cleopatra was also familiar with cold cream, the oldest cosmetic known to history.

1. You can conclude that
   (A) Strauss did not use denim to make his first pair of pants.
   (B) jeans today are made of canvas.
   (C) jeans are sold exclusively in New York and California.
   (D) blue jeans are one of the most popular types of pants in the world.

2. The story hints that there may
   (A) still exist a great number of schooners.
   (B) soon be a second great age of sailing ships.
   (C) be little interest in the port.
   (D) still exist whaling ships made of other materials.

3. A Pyrrhic victory is
   (A) unexpected.
   (B) not worth the price.
   (C) won by accident.
   (D) unfair.

4. From the story you can tell that
   (A) both miles are the same.
   (B) the statute mile is longer.
   (C) the nautical mile is longer.
   (D) travel is faster on land.

5. Cosmetics have been used since ancient times to
   (A) straighten hair.
   (B) aid health.
   (C) heal people.
   (D) improve appearance.

Unit 16

1.　　Ships that carry freight but do not travel on regular runs are called "tramps." A tramp steamer has no fixed schedule. It wanders from port to port. Declining in numbers in recent years, tramp steamers are seldom seen. When the last tramp steamer has made its final port call, a little of the traditional sailing days will have vanished.

2.　　The rhinoceros is regarded by hunters as one of the most dangerous animals in the world. Despite its size, the animal gallops along at 25 to 35 miles an hour. Its horn gives it a formidable weapon. What is worse, the rhino has poor eyesight and is easily startled. Without warning, the tanklike creature will charge!

3.　　Elephants display surprising intelligence. In the London Zoo, elephants were separated from the public buy two fences. Sometimes peanuts thrown by visitors landed between these fences, beyond the reach of both the people and the elephants. With a blast of air from their trunks, the elephants simply blew the peanuts back to the crowd so the visitors could try their toss again!

4.　　The English language did not originate in England. The language that became known as English was apparently first spoken by people living in what is now Germany. Tribes from this area brought their language with them when they invaded England. When we hear this early English, known as Anglo-Saxon or Old English, it is hard to believe that it was the ancestor of Modern English. It sounds more like German.

5.　　The flu, or influenza, has been around for centuries. Its name reminds us that people once looked to the sky for its cause. The word **influenza** comes from the Italian word for **influence** because people blamed their aches and fevers on the influence of the stars. In modern times scientists have found a better explanation by looking through a microscope. The flu is caused by a tiny form of matter called a virus.

1. You can tell that the writer thinks that
   (A) there will always be some tramp steamers.
   (B) the end of tramp steamers is no loss.
   (C) tramp steamers should have a schedule.
   (D) tramp steamers will one day be no more.

2. The story gives
   (A) ten reasons hunters fear the rhino.
   (B) at least three reasons the rhino is dangerous.
   (C) the reason for the rhino's poor eyesight.
   (D) a complete list of the rhino's habits.

3. From the story you cannot tell
   (A) that visitors had peanuts.
   (B) how many fences were there.
   (C) how many peanuts were lost.
   (D) how the elephants returned the peanuts.

4. The writer suggests that without early German tribes
   (A) there would be no written language.
   (B) the English language would be different today.
   (C) there would be no English people.
   (D) England would have no language.

5. From the story you can tell that
   (A) a virus can be seen with the naked eye.
   (B) the stars once caused sickness.
   (C) the author believes in scientific explanations.
   (D) a cure for the flu has been discovered.

1. The "World's Greatest Fair" in St. Louis, Missouri, began in 1904. This was the first fair of its kind. It marked the 100th anniversary of the Louisiana Purchase. This fair was open for nearly seven months and attracted more than 12 million people from around the world. Nearly 40 different countries had displays. The Liberty Bell was also on display. Even the 1904 Summer Olympic Games were played at the fair.

2. Some of the largest fires in history were started by seemingly insignificant accidents. In 1835 the great fire of New York City was started by stray sparks from a stove. Two days later the fire was under control, but more than 15 blocks of the Wall Street area had been consumed. Almost 700 buildings lay in ruins. The damage was estimated at 20 to 40 million dollars, which would be more than 300 million dollars today.

3. Airplanes have rules that govern the right-of-way in the sky. If two planes are flying so that their paths would cross, the plane to the right has the right-of-way. If two planes are flying toward one another, both pilots must fly their planes to the right. Airplanes must always give gliders and balloons the right-of-way.

4. When it is in danger, the hedgehog can usually protect itself by rolling into a tight ball. Completely surrounded by its own sharp spines, it is safe from most animals. A fox, however, may outsmart the hedgehog by rolling it into water. The hedgehog must then unroll itself to swim, leaving its underside open to attack by the fox.

5. On an island near Sicily is a volcano named Stromboli. The island itself bears the same name. There is more affection for Stromboli than there usually is for a volcano. Stromboli erupts every 15 to 20 minutes. For thousands of years it has been a guide to ships at sea. It has rightfully earned the title "Lighthouse of the Mediterranean Sea."

1. From the paragraph you can tell that
   (A) the World's Fair takes place every four years.
   (B) the 1904 World's Fair took place in New York City.
   (C) the World's Fair brought together people from many countries.
   (D) the Liberty Bell was made at the World's Fair.

2. You can tell that the fire
   (A) was easy to control.
   (B) didn't cause a lot of damage.
   (C) required few firefighters.
   (D) was hard to control.

3. Air and auto traffic are alike because
   (A) neither is dangerous.
   (B) only single-lane traffic is allowed.
   (C) they both have traffic laws.
   (D) each has speed laws.

4. From the story you can tell that a hedgehog
   (A) rolls into a ball to keep warm.
   (B) uses its spines to threaten its enemies.
   (C) is a poor swimmer.
   (D) does not have spines on its underside.

5. Stromboli is liked because it
   (A) is a volcano.
   (B) is nice and warm.
   (C) is helpful.
   (D) sends out lava.

1. Long ago, passenger pigeons flew over North America in such vast numbers that they actually darkened the sun as they passed. In a single flock there could be two billion passenger pigeons! The largest nesting area was one mile wide and three hundred miles long. Today the passenger pigeon is extinct. The last survivor of the breed died at the Cincinnati Zoo in 1914.

2. In 1959 a British engineer invented a transportation machine called the hovercraft. It is a boat-shaped, flat-bottomed carrier that rides on a cushion of air created by motors. One special feature of the hovercraft is its ability to ride over land and water at heights low enough for easy viewing. This has been useful in the exploration of rivers such as the Amazon.

3. The most beautiful of all horses is the Asil Arabian. Its neck is gracefully arched. Its head is small and delicate with eyes that are large, fiery, and far apart. Its small ears point inward. This horse has a full, flowing tail that it carries high, and its hair has a beautiful shine. The Asil Arabian is one of the most beautiful of all creatures.

4. The area that birds defend against other birds of their own species is called a territory. By controlling such an area, the bird protects its family from other birds of the same species. It is also ensured both food and nesting materials in this way. The size of the territory depends on many factors, such as the amount of food available, the type of bird, and even its size.

5. Sometimes the best inventions are accidents. In 1968 chemist Spencer Silver was trying to make a better adhesive for tape. Instead he created one that would not stick permanently. He knew the adhesive had potential, but he did not know what to do with it. Years later coworker Art Fry, annoyed that his bookmarks kept falling out of place, realized a use for the adhesive. The first sticky notes were born.

1. From the story you cannot tell
   (A) how large the flocks were.
   (B) when the passenger pigeon became extinct.
   (C) why the passenger pigeon died.
   (D) where the last passenger pigeon died.

2. From the story you can tell that the hovercraft
   (A) could be used for exploring a chain of islands.
   (B) resembles a helicopter.
   (C) is unsafe in stormy weather.
   (D) creates less noise and pollution than an automobile.

3. A good name for the Asil Arabian would be
   (A) Star of the North.
   (B) Brown Eyes.
   (C) Speedy.
   (D) Beauty.

4. The story gives
   (A) ten reasons for bird territories.
   (B) the writer's opinion of birds.
   (C) three factors for the size of bird territories.
   (D) the size of most bird territories in the United States.

5. All inventions
   (A) cost a lot of money.
   (B) require lots of time.
   (C) are not practical.
   (D) are not planned.

1. Walking on the wing of an airplane in flight was all in a day's work to Mabel Cody. This star of an aerial circus wore no parachute. Graceful, sure-footed Mabel Cody stood on the top of the upper wing of an airplane. As the air blasted against her, Mabel excitedly waved her arms to the crowds who gazed up at her in awe.

_____

2. The yo-yo, whose name means "come-come" or "to return," was first brought to the United States in the 1920s by a Philippine man named Pedro Flores. The yo-yo had already been a popular toy in the Philippines for many years. Flores settled in California and began carving yo-yos out of wood. Eventually he started a yo-yo company.

_____

3. The world's highest waterfall is not Niagara Falls. The highest waterfall lies deep in the jungles of Venezuela and is more than 1,000 feet higher than any other yet found. Named Angel Falls, after its American discoverer Jimmy Angel, the waterfall is almost a mile high. Its nearest competitor is the Kukenaam Falls, which is also in Venezuela.

_____

4. The rhinoceros, one of the world's most dangerous animals, gets along very well with a small bird that perches on its back. The bird, the tickbird, removes and eats potentially harmful insects from the back of the rhino. In exchange for its free meal, the tickbird also acts as an early warning system for the rhino. If the bird suddenly takes flight, the rhinoceros knows danger lurks nearby.

_____

5. Lacrosse is the oldest organized sport played in North America. This fast, rough game was played originally by Huron Indians. Early French and English settlers, after watching the Huron Indians play, adopted the game and made some changes in the rules. In modern lacrosse, players using long, net-ended sticks try to hurl a ball into the opposing team's goal area.

Unit 19

1. You can tell that Mabel Cody
   (A) had a good sense of balance.
   (B) was rather cautious.
   (C) loved all kinds of people.
   (D) was scared of heights.

2. The story suggests that Pedro Flores
   (A) invented the yo-yo.
   (B) started the first American yo-yo company.
   (C) had sold yo-yos in the Philippines before 1920.
   (D) named the yo-yo.

3. From the story you can tell that
   (A) Niagara Falls is the world's third-highest falls.
   (B) Angel Falls is not as high as Kukenaam Falls.
   (C) Angel Falls is higher than Niagara or Kukenaam Falls.
   (D) Angel Falls is only 1,000 feet high.

4. The story tells
   (A) four services the tickbird provides.
   (B) two services the tickbird provides.
   (C) the reasons why rhinos are dangerous.
   (D) what danger exists for rhinos.

5. From the story you can tell that
   (A) lacrosse is North America's most popular game.
   (B) early settlers learned from the Huron Indians.
   (C) no changes have ever been made in lacrosse.
   (D) all people played lacrosse.

A. Exercising Your Skill

A good detective uses clues to draw a conclusion about a crime. A good reader uses clues provided by the writer to draw a conclusion about a piece of writing. How good of a detective are you? Read each of the sets of clues below. On your paper write what you think happened in each case.

EVENT 1

Girl Scouts	tents	campfire
long pants	cold stream	sleeping bags
mosquitoes buzzing	moonless night	clearing in woods

What do you think happened?

EVENT 2

row of footprints	gray dust	silence
weightlessness	space suits	empty landscape
Earth shining above	rocks and craters	black sky

What do you think happened?

EVENT 3

crisp fall day	football field	teams running off
Visitors: 7	Home: 10	football held high
coach on shoulders	cheering crowd	banners waving

What do you think happened?

B. Expanding Your Skill

Compare the conclusions you drew about each event with your classmates' conclusions. Did everyone arrive at the same conclusions? Why or why not? Discuss the clues that led to each conclusion. What other clues might have helped you draw that conclusion? On your paper write additions to the list for each event.

C. Exploring Language

On page 48 you drew conclusions about an event that was based on nine facts. Let's see how good you are at drawing conclusions based on just three facts! Read each of the following items. Based on the overheard bits of conversation, tell what is happening.

1. "Get those ladders up there!" "Hoses on!" "Flames are on the top floor!"

2. "It's almost time for the show to start." "Look at that line at the ticket booth!" "Do you want to get some popcorn?"

3. "The Flying Estradas will now perform their own version of the triple somersault!" "Drum roll, please!" "He's going to fall! Oh, I can't bear to watch!"

4. "Forty-second Street! This station is 42nd Street." "Excuse me. Coming through." "Watch your step, please, and stay clear of the track."

5. "Please deposit 35 cents for the next three minutes." "Operator, I have no more change!" "This is a recording."

6. "Come, Sandy." "Exercise over. You can praise your dog now." "Good boy, Sandy!"

7. "Look! Bases loaded!" "How many outs?" "Maybe she'll hit a grand-slam homer!"

8. "Open your test booklets and begin." "Answer all the questions." "No talking!"

D. Expressing Yourself

Choose one of these activities.

1. Work together with a group of classmates to plan and act out a scene. (This can be one of the events based on the clues in Part C.) Have your other classmates draw a conclusion about what is happening. Ask them to explain their thoughts.

2. Make up a list of clues about an event. Then trade lists with a classmate. Write a few sentences that draw a conclusion about your classmate's list.

3. Write a short description of an area inside or near your school or of a well-known place in your town or city—but *don't* name it. Then exchange papers with a partner. Name the place your partner described. Was your guess correct? Did your partner correctly guess the place you described?

1.   In the early 1890s a teacher named James Naismith was asked to think up an active game that could be played indoors during the winter. Taking ideas from a game called Duck-on-a-Rock, Naismith invented the first version of basketball. The court was a YMCA gym with peach baskets nailed to the balcony. When a player made a basket, play would stop while someone climbed a ladder to take the ball out of the basket.

2.   The most unusual member of the deer family is the Florida key deer. Even when fully grown, it is North America's smallest deer. Fires, hurricanes, and hunters have killed many of these deer. The main reason the key deer are endangered is the loss of habitat due to human development.

3.   Some birds have an amazing ability to find their eggs after a storm. Terns, for example, nest on sandy ground, often laying two or three eggs in a shallow hole. Repeated observations have shown that even though the eggs are completely concealed by windblown sand, adult terns can easily find them.

4.   In drastically cold temperatures, ocean waters can be covered with thick layers of ice. Regular ocean liners cannot travel these ice-covered areas. Help comes in the form of powerful icebreaker ships. These ships are designed to push through and break the ice, leaving an open passageway for the ocean liners.

5.   Diamonds are now mined from the ocean floor. Walls are built to hold back the water. The sand is bulldozed aside until the diamond-bearing level is reached. The earth containing the diamonds is then taken to screening plants. The yield is much greater than from that on land. Furthermore, the diamonds from the seabed are often of higher quality.

1. From the story you cannot tell that
   (A) basketball has changed since the first game.
   (B) the bottoms were not cut out of the first baskets.
   (C) basketball has been around for about 100 years.
   (D) the walls of the gym were the first boundaries.

2. The writer suggests that
   (A) the deer get sick.
   (B) the deer love hurricanes.
   (C) people are destroying their habitat.
   (D) key deer are the largest deer.

3. The story doesn't tell
   (A) where terns lay eggs.
   (B) how many eggs terns lay.
   (C) how terns can find the eggs.
   (D) what windblown sand does to eggs.

4. You can tell from the story
   (A) how thick the ice is.
   (B) that the passageways are narrow.
   (C) why icebreaker ships are needed.
   (D) how cold the ocean is.

5. You can tell from the paragraph that
   (A) diamond mining is easy.
   (B) diamonds were once mined only on land.
   (C) mining is dangerous.
   (D) screening plants are far away.

1.   The life of the mayfly is pretty tough. It exists undeveloped in water for many months, perhaps a year. This length of time increases the mayfly's chances of being gobbled up by fish. Few mayflies survive long enough to leave the water. On land the mayfly reaches adulthood, mates, lays its eggs, and dies—all within 24 hours of leaving the water!

2.   Soap is now considered a mark of cultured living. As important as soap is to us today, it was all but unknown until about 2,000 years ago. Before people knew about soap, they scraped dirt from their bodies with twigs or an instrument known as a strigil. In still other times, people cleaned themselves with olive oil or plant juices.

3.   A virus is a microscopic organism that cannot do anything by itself. It has to invade a living cell, where it causes diseases such as the flu or a cold. Computer viruses are much the same. They can enter a computer and infect a program that is running. Then they take over or interfere with the normal processes of the computer, just as illnesses interfere with the health of humans.

4.   In the summer you can find out the temperature without listening to the weather station or looking at a thermometer. Just go outside to a quiet place, and listen to the crickets. Count the number of times the crickets chirp in 15 seconds. Then add 37 to that number. The sum will be very close to the actual temperature.

5.   Pound for pound, few creatures can match the appetite of the platypus of Australia. This strange creature looks like a combination of a muskrat and a duck. It weighs only two to four pounds. Yet it is so active that it must eat huge meals. In a single day it can eat an amount that is 15 percent to 30 percent of its body weight!

1. The writer seems to feel that the mayfly's adult life is
   (A) just like our lives.
   (B) not worth the wait.
   (C) worth waiting for.
   (D) more exciting than ours.

2. People of earlier times
   (A) were interested in cleanliness.
   (B) took showers every day.
   (C) didn't like soap.
   (D) knew much about soap.

3. You can conclude from this paragraph that
   (A) computer viruses can cause colds.
   (B) computer programmers often get the flu.
   (C) computer viruses are living things.
   (D) computer viruses are powerless by themselves.

4. The story does *not* suggest that
   (A) this method is used only in the summer.
   (B) crickets chirp faster as the temperature rises.
   (C) this method was used before thermometers existed.
   (D) this method is exact.

5. The platypus has few rivals in
   (A) intelligence.
   (B) activity.
   (C) beauty.
   (D) appetite.

1.   Except for the Italians, most people in Europe once considered tomatoes unsafe to eat. They believed that tomatoes would chill the body and cause illness. The British planted them only for their beauty. On the other hand South Americans had been eating them for centuries. In the 1800s the other European countries joined the Italians in using tomatoes as food.

2.   Many people think that they know why leaves change color in the fall. They say it is because of frost. Actually, the color changes because of the reduced amount of sunlight. This results in a slowdown in the production of chlorophyll, which is dark green. With less chlorophyll, other colors are able to shine through.

3.   One of the first elephants brought to America was Old Bet. She arrived in the early 1800s. Her owner had paid $1,000 for her. He wanted to exhibit her for money and did not want anyone to get a free look at his prize. How did he solve his problem? He and Old Bet walked country roads at night so that no one could see them.

4.   Most of the 2,700,000 soldiers in the Union army during the Civil War were between 18 and 39 years old. More than one million were 18. About 100,000 were 15 or younger. Some 300 soldiers were 13 or younger. These youngest soldiers were usually fifers and drummers, but sometimes they also fought.

5.   Long before an earthquake occurs, many animals seem to sense its approach. Cattle and sheep refuse to enter their pens. Rats flee their homes, and pigeons will not land. Fish leap above the surface of the water as if they would feel safer in the air. Even snakes that sleep through the winter wake up and leave their burrows. No one is sure what signals the animals to the danger.

1. You can tell that Europeans in the 1800s
   (A) first began planting tomatoes.
   (B) were introduced to tomatoes by South Americans.
   (C) grew sick from eating tomatoes.
   (D) learned that tomatoes were not unhealthful.

2. The more chlorophyll that leaves have, the
   (A) more frost there is.
   (B) less sunlight there is.
   (C) greener they are.
   (D) more quickly they change colors.

3. You can tell that
   (A) elephants were common in the early 1800s.
   (B) Old Bet would earn money as a curiosity.
   (C) Old Bet's owner did not like people.
   (D) people had seen many elephants.

4. Most of the Union army soldiers were
   (A) musicians.
   (B) 15 years old.
   (C) under 40 years old.
   (D) unreliable.

5. From the story you cannot tell whether
   (A) animals feel or hear earthquake vibrations.
   (B) animals prefer open spaces before an earthquake.
   (C) animal behavior can warn people of earthquakes.
   (D) wild animals can sense approaching earthquakes.

1.   On the island of Molokai in Hawaii is a rubber-bottomed lake. It is a human-made lake that holds water for irrigating the fields where pineapple and other crops grow. Such a lake is called a reservoir. This reservoir had to have a huge rubber bottom installed. Otherwise the water would leak away into the ground. Now farmers on Molokai have enough water to raise good crops.

2.   In the early days of Texas, the famed longhorn cattle were valued more for their hides than for their meat. Rawhide provided a valuable building material in the old West. Hides were used in binding beams and fence rails, and in making furniture. Even items of clothing were made of rawhide—boots, shoes, trousers, and jackets. In the absence of other building materials, Texans found rawhide to be a valuable substitute.

3.   Hurricane hunters are always on the alert for those storms that whip out of the Caribbean with destructive force. The hurricane hunters' planes circle the storm area, getting readings on the hurricane's size, its strength, and the direction in which it is moving. Small radio transmitters are dropped into the storm centers by parachute and relay important information back to the plane.

4.   In the 18th century, people often rode in a "ride-and-tie" fashion. Two people got on the horse, one behind the other, while another couple walked. After a mile or two, the riders got off the horse, tied it to a tree, and began to walk. The first couple, when they came to the horse, would ride a mile or two past the other couple, tie up the horse, and start walking again.

5.   The word **skate** is taken from a Dutch word meaning "leg bone." Ice skates have been used for more than 2,000 years. A Viking boot and skate from the tenth century have been found. The boot is not attached to the skate, however. The skater's weight probably kept the boot in place.

1. You can tell that this part of Molokai
   (A) has many rubber trees.
   (B) gets very heavy rainfall.
   (C) needs extra water for farming.
   (D) is below sea level.

2. You can tell that the hides
   (A) were expensive.
   (B) had a good taste.
   (C) had more uses than the meat.
   (D) wore out quickly.

3. Hurricane hunters must be
   (A) strong.
   (B) pilots.
   (C) fighters.
   (D) big.

4. By using this method
   (A) the horse got a ride.
   (B) each person rode all the way.
   (C) even the horse got a rest.
   (D) each person walked all the way.

5. This paragraph suggests that
   (A) Vikings did not skate before the tenth century.
   (B) the first materials used for boots were animal skins.
   (C) the Dutch have no word for *boot*.
   (D) today's boots and skates are attached.

Unit 24

1. Dinosaurs swallowed stones to help them digest their food. (Chickens do this also.) The juices inside the dinosaurs' stomachs made the stone smooth and shiny over a period of time. These stones are sometimes called gizzard stones or gastroliths. Naturally they are prized by fossil collectors.

2. Those who want to learn more about the life of Helen Keller should visit Tuscumbia, Alabama, her birthplace. Each summer, William Gibson's play, *The Miracle Worker,* is staged. This play dramatizes the story of Helen Keller, who was blind and deaf from the age of two. The story of her courage and the efforts of her teacher and companion, Anne Sullivan, provide audiences with an unforgettable experience.

3. The most famous rock in America lies on the seashore at Plymouth, Massachusetts, under the protection of a large granite canopy. According to legend, the Pilgrims stepped from their ship, the *Mayflower,* onto this rock when they landed on December 21, 1620. Today people come from all over America to see this famous rock, which stands as a symbol of the Pilgrims' courage.

4. In the Asian country of Sri Lanka is an orphanage for baby elephants. The babies are fed milk from a rubber hose that is attached to a bottle. Every morning they walk down a path to the river, and children from the village walk along with them. At the river the elephants bathe and play in the water.

5. One of the truly great agricultural expositions in America is held during August on a 200-acre fairground in Des Moines, Iowa. The Iowa State Fair, which dates back more than 150 years, attracts more than a million visitors annually. Young and old are enlightened and entertained by contests, demonstrations, agricultural and industrial exhibits, horse shows, auto races, and fireworks.

1. From the story you can tell
   (A) that dinosaurs and chickens have nothing in common.
   (B) why dinosaurs swallowed stones.
   (C) that dinosaur meat was delicious.
   (D) that the stones were swallowed by accident.

2. *The Miracle Worker* is probably
   (A) a long play.
   (B) a dull play.
   (C) an inspiring play.
   (D) a three-act play.

3. Plymouth Rock is
   (A) larger than the *Mayflower*.
   (B) a reminder of our history.
   (C) not well known.
   (D) a famous amusement center.

4. From the story you cannot tell
   (A) how the elephants are fed.
   (B) what the elephants eat.
   (C) how the elephants became orphans.
   (D) that the elephants enjoy the river.

5. From the story you can tell that
   (A) the Iowa Fair is for Iowans only.
   (B) the Iowa Fair appeals to different people.
   (C) the Iowa Fair does not have exhibitions.
   (D) farmers would not enjoy the Iowa Fair.

1.   One of our five senses needs help to work well. The tongue can sense only four tastes—sweet, sour, bitter, and salty. Taste alone cannot tell one sweet thing from another, such as honey and syrup. We depend also on what each looks like, smells like, and feels like in our mouth.

2.   Inventors are often very observant. One day Percy Spencer was standing in front of a magnetron, an electronic tube that produces microwaves. It was developed during World War II for use in radar systems. The chocolate bar Spencer had in his pocket melted as he stood there, and he wondered if microwaves could be used for cooking. They could. The first such oven was patented in 1946.

3.   People have been ice-skating in northern Europe for more than 2,000 years. The earliest skate blades were made of animal bones. Later they were made of wood, then iron, and now steel. Ice-skating first became popular in the Netherlands. There the country's network of canals became highways of ice in the winter, and people could skate to work or school.

4.   "To go high-hat" means to become a snob and look down on your friends. Long ago people who suddenly became wealthy often wore silly high hats. They ignored the old friends that they had when they were poor. Their high hats became signs of their newfound wealth, hence the expression "to go high-hat."

5.   The overland coaches that rolled across America in the early 1800s were not only fashioned with craftsmanship, they were also attractive. Pictures were painted on each door, most often landscapes or portraits of famous people. Even the wheels were decorated with handsome stripes.

1. If you closed your eyes and held your nose, it would be hardest to tell the difference between swallowing
   (A) sugar and salt.
   (B) canned pears and canned potatoes.
   (C) a pickle slice and a banana slice.
   (D) grape juice and pineapple juice.

2. You can conclude from this paragraph that
   (A) Percy Spencer was a war hero.
   (B) Percy Spencer invented the chocolate bar.
   (C) Percy Spencer invented the magnetron.
   (D) Percy Spencer invented the microwave oven.

3. Skating became popular in the Netherlands because
   (A) the winters were so long and cold.
   (B) skate blades had been improved.
   (C) it was a handy means of transportation.
   (D) the frozen canals made smooth skating surfaces.

4. People can go high-hat because of
   (A) the poor.
   (B) their friends.
   (C) their neighbors.
   (D) money.

5. You can tell that the overland coaches were
   (A) attractively designed.
   (B) very roomy.
   (C) often in need of repair.
   (D) not often used.

A. Exercising Your Skill

A conclusion is a decision or judgment you make that is based on facts and information. Syllogisms help organize information so that readers can draw a conclusion based on facts. In a syllogism all the information you need to draw a conclusion is given in two statements called premises. Read the two syllogisms below. Note the underlined words and the letters above them. Think about the premises in each syllogism. The first syllogism is correct; the second is incorrect.

	Syllogism 1	**Syllogism 2**
First premise:	A B All horses eat hay.	A B All horses eat hay.
Second premise:	C A Jingle is a horse.	C B A deer eats hay.
Conclusion:	C B Jingle eats hay.	C A A deer is a horse.

Using the patterns AB, CA, and CB as guides and thinking about the premises will help you recognize a correct syllogism.

Now read each of the following syllogisms. On your paper write *Correct* if the syllogism is correct and *Incorrect* if it is incorrect.

1. First premise: All tarantulas are spiders.
   Second premise: All spiders have eight legs.
   Conclusion: Tarantulas have eight legs.

2. First premise: All languages have meaning.
   Second premise: The Russian language has meaning.
   Conclusion: All languages are Russian.

3. First premise: All snakes shed their skin.
   Second premise: A boa constrictor is a snake.
   Conclusion: A boa constrictor sheds its skin.

B. Expanding Your Skill

Discuss each syllogism with your classmates. If the syllogism is correct, explain how the premises led to the conclusion. If the syllogism is incorrect, explain the error that was made. On your paper rewrite any incorrect syllogism to make it correct.

C. Exploring Language

Read each of the following syllogisms. For each pair of premises, write the correct conclusion on your paper.

1. First premise: All felines have whiskers.
   Second premise: A lion is a feline.
   Conclusion:

2. First premise: All citrus fruits contain vitamin C.
   Second premise: An orange is a citrus fruit.
   Conclusion:

3. First premise: Only a native-born American can become president of the United States.
   Second premise: Bill Clinton was president of the United States from 1993 to 2001.
   Conclusion:

4. First premise: All reference books give factual information.
   Second premise: An encyclopedia is a reference book.
   Conclusion:

5. First premise: Only living things can breathe.
   Second premise: A rock is not a living thing.
   Conclusion:

D. Expressing Yourself

Choose one of these activities.

1. Using Part C as a guide, work in two teams to create syllogisms; omit the conclusion that can be drawn. Teams take turns reading their premises to the other team. A correct conclusion scores one point for the guessing team. An incorrect syllogism scores a point for the asking team.

2. On an index card write a conclusion. Exchange conclusions with a classmate, and write two premises that led to your classmate's conclusion. Share premises and conclusions with the rest of the class.

3. Think of a syllogism. Then get three index cards. On one card write the first premise; on the second card write the second premise; and on the third card write the conclusion. Mix up the cards. Ask your classmates to put the cards in order.